W9-BHP-937

WITHDRAWN

Native Americans

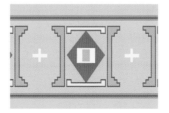

Arapaho

Barbara A. Gray-Kanatiiosh

ABDO Publishing Company

visit us at
www.abdopublishing.com

Printed in the United States.

Cover Photo: Marilyn "Angel" Wynn/Nativestock.com
Interior Photos: Corbis pp. 4, 30; Getty Images p. 30; Index Stock p. 29
Illustrations: David Kanietakeron Fadden pp. 7, 9, 11, 13, 15, 17, 19, 21, 23, 25, 27
Editors: Rochelle Baltzer, Megan Murphy
Art Direction & Maps: Neil Klinepier

Library of Congress Cataloging-in-Publication Data

Gray-Kanatiiosh, Barbara A., 1963-
  Arapaho / Barbara A. Gray-Kanatiiosh.
     p. cm. -- (Native Americans)
  Includes bibliographical references and index.
  ISBN-10 1-59197-649-9
  ISBN-13 978-1-59197-649-3
1. Arapaho Indians--History. 2. Arapaho Indians--Social life and customs. I. Title. II. Series: Native Americans (Edina, Minn.)

  E99.A7G63 2006
  978.004'97354--dc22

                                                                                   2004050165

About the Author: Barbara A. Gray-Kanatiiosh, JD

Barbara Gray-Kanatiiosh, JD, Ph.D. ABD, is an Akwesasne Mohawk. She resides at the Mohawk Nation and is of the Wolf Clan. She has a Juris Doctorate from Arizona State University, where she was one of the first recipients of ASU's special certificate in Indian Law. Barbara's Ph.D. is in Justice Studies at ASU. She is currently working on her dissertation, which concerns the impacts of environmental injustice on indigenous culture. Barbara works hard to educate children about Native Americans through her writing and Web site, where children may ask questions and receive a written response about the Haudenosaunee culture. The Web site is: www.peace4turtleisland.org

About the Illustrator: David Kanietakeron Fadden

David Kanietakeron Fadden is a member of the Akwesasne Mohawk Wolf Clan. His work has appeared in publications such as *Akwesasne Notes*, *Indian Time*, and the *Northeast Indian Quarterly*. Examples of his work have also appeared in various publications of the Six Nations Indian Museum in Onchiota, NY. His work has also appeared in "How the West Was Lost: Always the Enemy," produced by Gannett Production, which appeared on the Discovery Channel. David's work has been exhibited in Albany, NY; the Lake Placid Center for the Arts; Centre Strathearn in Montreal, Quebec; North Country Community College in Saranac Lake, NY; Paul Smith's College in Paul Smiths, NY; and at the Unison Arts & Learning Center in New Paltz, NY.

Contents

Where They Lived

The Arapaho (uh-RA-puh-hoh) originally called themselves *Inuna-ina*. This means "our people" in Arapaho, which is part of the Algonquian language family. The Cheyenne called their Arapaho **allies** *hitanwo'iv*, which means "people of the sky."

The Arapaho homelands were once located northeast of the Missouri River. Gradually, the Arapaho **migrated** west to the Great Plains. Parts of present-day Wyoming, Colorado, Kansas, and Nebraska were in this territory. Neighboring tribes included the Shoshone, Pawnee, Cheyenne, and Kiowa.

There were many different landforms in Arapaho territory. Rolling hills, grassy plains, vast canyons, open valleys, and towering mountains stretched across the area. Lakes, streams, ponds, marshes, and rivers also covered the land.

The Arapaho homelands were abundant with natural beauty.

Many types of plants and animals lived on Arapaho land. The area's plants included trees, shrubs, wildflowers, and berry bushes. The grassy plains were home to buffalo and prairie chickens. Pronghorn, deer, and elks were also found on the land. Smaller animals included rabbits, squirrels, beavers, and quail.

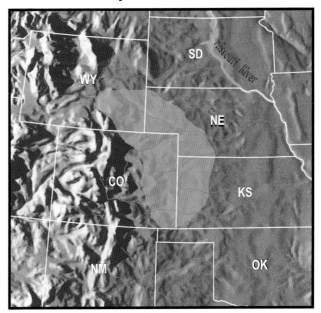

5

Society

The Arapaho lived in four bands that were nomadic. This means that they did not stay in one place for very long. During the summer, each band split into family groups. The groups returned to their winter villages to rejoin their bands.

Arapaho society depended on each person's contribution to the band. Every village had a chief. He got approval from everyone before he made a decision. And, he always considered the group's well-being.

In addition to the village chief, each band had priests. These men and women conducted ceremonies and **rituals**. During the rituals, they offered prayers of thanks. They also healed the Arapaho and protected them from harm.

Secret societies were another part of Arapaho life. The societies worked to protect the Arapaho people and their **culture**. Within each society, members were instructed in Arapaho traditions. Each person had special duties.

Each society had its own medicine bundle to care for. The bundle consisted of a sacred pipe, a wheel or hoop, and other important items. The Arapaho used these items for **rituals** or on special occasions.

The Arapaho often set up their villages in wooded areas along rivers.

Food

The Arapaho were hunters and gatherers. Nature provided them with food. The women and children gathered vegetables, fruits, seeds, roots, and nuts. They collected foods such as wild carrots, wild onions, and wild berries for their families.

The men hunted buffalo, elks, pronghorn, and deer. They also tracked rabbits, squirrels, beavers, prairie chickens, and quail. They hunted with traps, spears, knives, and bows and arrows.

Early buffalo hunting was difficult and unsafe. Hunters had to get close enough to a buffalo to cut its leg. Once the buffalo was hurt, the men killed it with a spear or a bow and arrow. Sometimes, the men chased buffalo off cliffs to kill them.

After the arrival of horses, buffalo hunting became less difficult. Around 1730, the Arapaho began using horses to separate a buffalo from its herd. This made the animal easier to kill. Then, the men butchered the buffalo and brought the meat back to camp.

The Arapaho used buffalo meat for soups and stews. The women prepared some meat for winter use. They cut it into pieces and dried it on racks. They mixed dried buffalo meat, **tallow**, and berries together to make pemmican. They ate pemmican during long trips and in the winter.

Arapaho women made soups and stews early in the morning. People ate the soups at any time of the day.

Homes

The Arapaho lived in tepees. Tepee size varied, but each home was large enough to hold one family. A family consisted of a mother, a father, and children. Sometimes, **extended family** members shared the same tepee.

Tepees were usually between 12 and 20 feet (4 and 6 m) tall. Women were in charge of building the tepees. First, they erected three wooden poles to make a triangle. Then, they added 20 to 30 more poles to form an upside-down cone.

Next, the women wrapped a cover made of buffalo hides around the frame. They fastened it at the front with wooden pins. Finally, they pounded wooden stakes through the bottom of the cover and into the ground. This made the home stable. A hide flap covered the entrance.

The Arapaho needed to protect their homes from winds and cold weather. So, women sometimes put soil on the outside of the tepee for warmth. The inside of the tepee had a special lining. The men painted on this lining to record hunts, wars, and special events.

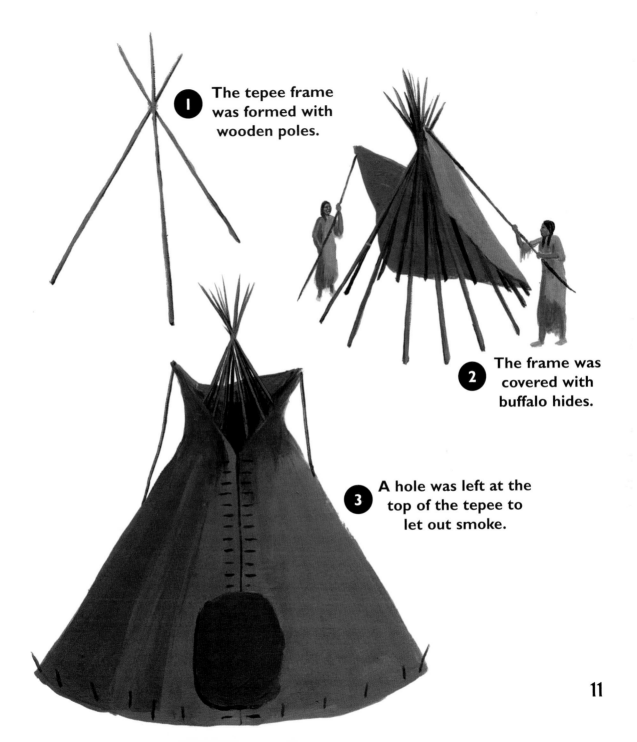

1 The tepee frame was formed with wooden poles.

2 The frame was covered with buffalo hides.

3 A hole was left at the top of the tepee to let out smoke.

11

Clothing

The Arapaho wore clothing made from deer and elk hides. The women used deer **sinew** and an **awl** to sew the hides together. Then, they decorated the clothing with porcupine **quillwork**, animal teeth, and horn and stone beads.

Men wore **breechcloths**, shirts, moccasins, and leggings. The leggings covered the legs to protect them from brush and thorns. Women wore fringed dresses and knee-length leggings. When the weather was cold, they wore moccasins that attached to the leggings.

During winter, the Arapaho wore robes made from buffalo hides. The side with hair was worn against the body. This trapped in heat and kept the body warm. The Arapaho used hides from buffalo taken in the autumn, when they have the thickest coat.

Tattoos were common among the Arapaho. Typically, a woman had a tattoo of a circle on her forehead. And, a man had a tattoo of a circle on his chest. To make tattoos, the Arapaho pricked their skin with a porcupine quill and rubbed in charcoal.

The Arapaho often designed their clothing using geometric shapes such as straight lines, circles, or triangles.

13

Crafts

The Arapaho were known for their elaborate **quillwork** and beadwork. They used beads and porcupine quills to decorate **awl** and knife **sheaths**. They also decorated clothing, moccasins, armbands, bags, and baby cradles.

The Arapaho designs were sacred. They came from legends and dreams. These designs were thought to protect the wearer. And, decorated baby cradles were believed to keep infants from harm.

Only women who belonged to a porcupine quill society were allowed to do quillwork. Within the society, elderly women taught young beginners the art of quilling. It took many years for women to perfect their quillwork.

There were many steps to quilling. First, women pulled quills from a porcupine hide. Then they cleaned, sorted, and dyed the quills. They made the dye from wild onion skins, wild berries, and roots. And, they stored the dyed quills in containers made from **untanned** hide.

The women used needles and **awls** made of bone to sew the quills onto clothing. And, they used thread made of buffalo **sinew**.

Elderly Arapaho women taught younger women quilling techniques.

Family

Men and women had specific jobs within Arapaho society. Each person was expected to help the band survive. Responsibilities and privileges usually depended on gender and age.

Hunting was a man's most important job. He was expected to provide meat for his family and his band. He also built tools and weapons. A man was ready to marry when he could prove his hunting skills. This showed that he would be able to provide for a family.

Traditionally, the Arapaho practiced arranged marriages. This meant that a woman's older brother, father, or uncle chose her husband. Typically, a woman got married in her late teens.

Before and after marriage, women had several important jobs. They gathered and prepared food, built tepees, and made clothing. Warm clothing was necessary for survival during the harsh winters. To make clothing, women scraped and **tanned** animal hides so they were soft enough to work with. They also made robes and tepee covers with the tanned hides.

Arapaho women scraped animal
hides with stone or bone tools.

Children

Arapaho elders taught children many useful things. They taught them traditional ceremonial songs, dances, and stories. Children helped with daily chores, such as gathering food and firewood. They also learned how to make bags from **untanned** hides.

Arapaho boys were taught how to hunt at a young age. They learned how to imitate animal calls, which they used to attract birds and other animals. Then, they could easily find and hunt those animals. A boy received his first pony as a young child. Boys learned how to become expert horse riders.

Women taught the girls how to tan animal hides. Girls learned how to sew the hides together with a bone **awl** and **sinew**. They also learned how to cook meals for their families.

In their free time, children played with toys together. They had fun playing with a buzz toy. This toy was made with a flat piece of bone. The bone was tied on each end with sinew. Each piece of sinew had a small wooden handle attached. When children pulled the handles, it made the bone spin and buzz.

It was important that a boy learned to ride a horse. So traditionally, an Arapaho father gave his son a pony.

Myths

The Arapaho use myths to help people understand many things about life. They share many stories about Sky World, a world found high above the trees.

One day, a man who lived in Sky World stumbled upon a hole. From the hole, he saw a camp of tepees. He noticed an Arapaho woman sitting in a **quillwork** circle. He watched her use porcupine quills to create beautiful designs. Instantly, he fell in love, and he wanted to marry her. So, he transformed himself into a porcupine and went down to Earth.

"Look at the beautiful quills on that porcupine," the woman said when she saw the porcupine man. "I am going to catch him." She left the quill circle and chased him up a tree. As she climbed, the tree grew taller.

Soon the woman reached Sky World, and the porcupine turned back into a man. He told the woman that he was in love with her, and soon they were married. But, the Arapaho woman missed her family and friends. So, she wove a **sinew** rope so she could return to Earth. She went to the hole in the sky and used the rope to lower herself. But the rope was too short.

A passing buzzard carried her on his back. Soon, the buzzard became tired and asked a hawk for help. So, the hawk took the woman on his back and brought her safely home. Today, the Arapaho leave an offering of thanks for the buzzard and the hawk.

The Arapaho woman returned to Earth through the hole in Sky World.

War

The Arapaho warred against several hostile tribes, including the Ute, Crow, Kiowa, and Comanche. And, they joined forces with other tribes, such as the Cheyenne, to attack the Sioux.

The tools used for hunting were also used as weapons. Among these were bows and arrows, knives, and spears. The bows were carved from cedar and rubbed with **tallow**. Thin strips of **sinew** were wrapped around the bow to make it strong. The arrows and spears had stone arrowheads attached with sinew. The knives were carved from a buffalo's shoulder blade.

The Arapaho wore bone armor for protection. They made breastplates with long beads carved from buffalo bone or horn. This protected their chests. Arrows, knives, and spears reflected off their armor.

The Arapaho also made shields from **untanned** hide. They used buffalo hide because it was very strong. Warriors often painted designs on their shields. They believed the designs would protect them during battle.

After the arrival of horses, warfare increased. Horses became a symbol of wealth. And, they enabled the Arapaho to travel farther. Many tribes, including the Arapaho, began to steal horses from each other.

Arapaho warriors carried decorated shields. The designs usually came from visions or dreams.

Contact with Europeans

European traders made contact with the Arapaho in the 1600s. French trader Jean Baptiste Trudeau spoke with the Arapaho in 1795. And in the 1800s, American traders came to the Great Plains in search of furs.

The Arapaho traded furs for manufactured goods. They received glass beads, wool cloth, cooking pots, and tobacco. They also received weapons such as iron arrowheads, metal knives, axes, and guns.

After 1830, the Arapaho split into two groups. Those that moved north became the Northern Arapaho tribe. And, those that moved south became the Southern Arapaho tribe.

In 1858, gold was discovered in Colorado. Soon after, a flood of settlers and miners came to Southern Arapaho territory. Many of them attacked the Arapaho and took animals. This caused the buffalo to become scarce.

In 1864, Colonel John M. Chivington led a surprise attack on the Arapaho and Cheyenne. Chivington and his group attacked a peaceful camp called Sand Creek. About 150 Arapaho and Cheyenne people died that day. Today, it is known as the Sand Creek Massacre.

Jean Baptiste Trudeau spoke with the Arapaho and recorded information about them.

Niwot

Niwot was a respected Southern Arapaho leader and speaker. He supported peaceful relations with other tribes and traders. He was born during the early 1820s. *Niwot* means "left hand." He was given the name at a young age because he was left-handed.

Niwot learned English from his sister's husband who was a trader. In 1858, Niwot surprised gold miners when he spoke their language. His ability to speak English helped him become a famous Arapaho leader.

The Southern Arapaho tribe was interested in protecting trade relations with the Europeans and the U.S. government. Niwot often worked with Little Raven, who was the principle chief of the Southern Arapaho. Together, they tried to establish peace with the United States.

In 1864, Niwot and his group were at Sand Creek when Colonel Chivington and his group attacked the camp. Niwot was fatally wounded, and he died soon after.

Niwot was a famous Arapaho leader.

The Arapaho Today

In the late 1800s and early 1900s, the U.S. government hoped to end Native American tribal traditions. So, the government passed **assimilation** laws. These laws forced Native Americans to adapt to European **cultural** ways.

To do this, the United States sent Arapaho children to boarding schools. Some children were sent far from their homes. They missed their families. The federal government also passed laws that made it a crime for Native Americans to gather together. The Arapaho were not allowed to dance or conduct ceremonies.

Today, the Arapaho take pride in their culture and traditions. Every year, the Northern and Southern Arapaho gather to celebrate the sun dance ceremony. This event takes place at the Wind River **Reservation** in July or August and lasts for seven days. It is a sacred time of praying, dancing, singing, and eating.

Currently, there are about 7,000 Arapaho tribal members. They live on **federally recognized** Arapaho reservations. The Northern Arapaho and the Shoshone live on the Wind River Reservation in Wyoming. The Southern Arapaho share a reservation with the Cheyenne in Oklahoma.

This Cheyenne Arapaho family is dressed in traditional powwow clothing.

Arapaho tribal members celebrated the opening of the Smithsonian National Museum of the American Indian on September 21, 2004.

Arapaho Cassie Soldierwolf (right) performed the butterfly dance at the American Indian Dance Theater in 1992.

Glossary

allies - people or countries that agree to help each other in times of need.

assimilate - to become a comfortable part of a new culture or society.

awl - a pointed tool for making small holes in materials such as leather or wood.

breechcloth - a piece of hide or cloth, usually worn by men, that wraps between the legs and ties with a belt around the waist.

culture - the customs, arts, and tools of a nation or people at a certain time.

extended family - a family that includes grandparents, uncles, aunts, and cousins in addition to a mother, father, and children.

federal recognition - the U.S. government's recognition of a tribe as being an independent nation. The tribe is then eligible for special funding and for protection of its reservation lands.

migrate - to move from one place to another, often to find food.

quillwork - the use of porcupine quills to make designs on clothing or cradleboards.

reservation - a piece of land set aside by the government for Native Americans to live on.

ritual - a form or order to a ceremony.

sheath - a leather holder used to store sharp objects.

sinew - a band of tough fibers that joins a muscle to a bone.

tallow - the melted fat of cattle and sheep.

tan - to make a hide into leather by soaking it in a special liquid.

tattoo - a permanent design made on the skin.

Web Sites

To learn more about the Arapaho, visit ABDO Publishing Company on the World Wide Web at **www.abdopub.com**. Web sites about the Arapaho are featured on our Book Links page. These links are routinely monitored and updated to provide the most current information available.

Index